Whimsical Sensations

TIM RIDSDALE

Suite 300 - 990 Fort St
Victoria, BC, V8V 3K2
Canada

www.friesenpress.com

Copyright © 2021 by Tim Ridsdale
First Edition — 2021

All rights reserved.

No part of this publication may be reproduced in any form, or by any means, electronic or mechanical, including photocopying, recording, or any information browsing, storage, or retrieval system, without permission in writing from FriesenPress.

ISBN
978-1-4602-3597-3 (Hardcover)
978-1-4602-3598-0 (Paperback)
978-1-4602-3599-7 (eBook)

1. POETRY, SUBJECTS & THEMES, LOVE & EROTICA

Distributed to the trade by The Ingram Book Company

I would like to thank Heather who encouraged me to write again and share it with the world.

I can feel your breath
When we are apart
I can feel the soft beat
Of the rhythm of your heart
I can feel your kisses
Against my skin
I can feel the contentment
That swells from within
I can feel your warmth
Against my side
I can hear your sighs
So sweetly amplified
I can feel your legs
Intertwined with mine
I can feel cold feet
When they serpentine
I can feel gentle fingers
Stroke through my hair
Softly they touch
Lighter than air
I can feel you my love
Even when you are far
You shine into my life
Like the evening star!

TIM RIDSDALE

When I hear your name
It's like the spring music of birds
Tickling my ears
With so many words
I see gentle and sweet
I see thoughtful and kind
I feel amazing love
No words have defined
I see a dedicated mother
I see family so strong
I feel amazing love
That could never go wrong
I see a hard-working lady
I see friendship's ideal
I feel amazing love
That's honest and real
But when I hear our names
Spoken together
My heart slowly melts
And I think of forever.

WHIMSICAL SENSATIONS

I fell in love with a butterfly
So beautiful and free
Spreading an amazing light
For everyone to see
From flower to flower
From beauty to love
Touching my life
Like a velvety glove
Leaving love to blossom
And my soul to soar
Submitting my heart
For your love to explore
No sounds but its beating
So softly for you
Like the wings of a butterfly
So gentle and true!

TIM RIDSDALE

Love will reach
Way down in our soul
Seep through our thoughts
As our hearts unfold
No matter the hurt
Or depth of the scar
Love's gentle caress
Reaches deep and far
It reminds us we're eagles
Meant to soar on the breeze
Above all the bondage
That drags us down on our knees
It awakens that light
That was forever sleeping
Breaking the chains
Of loneliness' keeping
When love comes gently
It brings tears of joy
To wash away memories
Of all hurt's employs
When love reaches out
With open arms
Embrace it fully
And all of its charms.

WHIMSICAL SENSATIONS

I want to watch the sunrise
With you in my arms
Feeling that love
In the soul that warms
Love's fruit is tender
And always in season
It brings out a passion
I can't logic or reason
I can feel your heat
As you get under my skin
So holding you closer
We invite love in
I can write secret notes
On your back as you sleep
For your soul to know
And your heart to keep
I will love you in such a way
You feel totally free
To find in yourself
The one you should be
To find love's essence
And eternal support
Pure as its gift
Strong as a Fort
With you in my arms
All must relent
To Love's gentle strength
That leaves us content.

TIM RIDSDALE

Love is not just words
Or a gentle emotion
It's passion in action
And deeper devotion
Love is more than a want
Or deep-seeded need
It's that first breath of air
When our soul is freed
Love is more than excitement
That builds like fire
It's those special moments
That feed our desire
So I will never steal
A single moment from you
But rather share them all
In life, love, and all that's true!

WHIMSICAL SENSATIONS

The light in my heart
That burns for you
Lights up my life
For my love to pursue
I love to sleep
In your warm embrace
The gentle rhythm of your heart
Brings peace and grace
Mornings come too fast
And days apart are long
But evening brings you back to me
Like the melody of that perfect song
That tickles our souls
And rests in our dreams
Filling our lives
Until they burst at the seams
To know your love
Is almost surreal
Even harder to express
Is all you make me feel
But in my arms
Everything is right
Burning in my heart
Your loves amazing light.

TIM RIDSDALE

The touch of my hand
Caressing your skin
Awakens your passion
And desires within
Burning kisses
On trembling lips
Gentle sweet touches
Of my fingertips
The look in your eyes
That says I'm your man
Leaves my heart soaring
In every way that it can
There is a spiritual closeness
That dances with my soul
Leaving me reeling
Challenging for control
The warmth of your breath
Against my chest
Leaves my heart
To what yours suggests
In the depth of the night
Or the light of the day
Your eyes still sparkle
And lead me away.

WHIMSICAL SENSATIONS

I wonder which is better
To share with you my love
The long cold nights of winter
Embraced tightly as a glove
Or maybe the warmth
Of the summer night
Lying there naked
For our own delight
Or maybe an evening
By the flames of the fireplace
Soft fingertip touches
Caressing your face
Or maybe on a blanket
Under the sweet summer sun
Laughing and teasing
Two lovers having fun
It really doesn't matter
The day or the weather
It's all so precious
To spend together.

TIM RIDSDALE

When I close my eyes
I see color and light
Splashed vibrantly together
Like a sailor's delight
That lights up the sky
Just before sunset
Like angels singing
In God's own quartet
These are not really dreams
But rather love's memory
Pulled from my thoughts
Deep in my own treasury
That replays your touch
Your soft gentle kiss
Lost in your arms
My heart loves to reminisce
While I rest at your side
Content with you near
My soul keeps talking
To you my dear!

WHIMSICAL SENSATIONS

You made me smile today
A little sunshine
In my busy day
Received so genuine
You lifted my spirit
With your loving smile
A place where warmth
Invited me to stay awhile
That perfect place
Where two lovers meet
Over morning coffee
Or on a quiet street
That gentle exchange
Lovers never miss
That leads us softly to
Another amazing kiss.

TIM RIDSDALE

To be born into love
That's how I feel
Such a peaceful state
That seems quite genteel
No we don't lack passion
Or a fiery start
We have all the desires
That fill our hearts
But with you there's beauty
That comes from within
Like a song from the soul
Of a Stradivarius violin
Your touch is heavenly
Your kisses divine
I get lost in the moment
Of love's deeper design
When hungry desire
Meets patience and calm

WHIMSICAL SENSATIONS

Like the flight of a butterfly
Resting safely in my palm
The heat of your body
Draws me closer at night
But it's in the light of the day
I face a greater plight
To want to be near you
To hug and laugh
All of these things
That fall short of a graph
You can't measure the power
That's stronger than oceans
You can't hardly explain
Love's depth of emotions
But it's there for the gentle
For the strong and the kind
All the sweetest treasures
In you I can find.

TIM RIDSDALE

I'm caught in your love
Wrapped up in your heat
The breath of your whisper
So tender and sweet
Like a breeze in the night
Caressing my skin
Expanding like fire
Pulsing deep from within
My body aches
For all you deliver
Coursing through my veins
In a passionate shiver
Like a fireworks show
You explode on my senses
Exciting and real
With no false pretenses
My yearning is quenched
In the sultry moment
Your sensual kiss
Is the missing component
You shake and you quiver
As our senses overload
In a wave of pure warmth
Together we explode
Left weak and diminished
Our souls laid bare
Yet the perfect emotions
We were able to share!

WHIMSICAL SENSATIONS

Your gentle sighs
Beckon me near
Searching your eyes
For the tiniest fear
But what I see
Is beautiful and bold
Stirring my soul
In all I hold
My hand fits perfectly
On the back of your neck
Like soft silky satin
It leaves my heart in check
Your eyes they sparkle
And your kiss beckons
Time slows down
Extending the seconds
Your warmth soothes me
Like a hot summer day
To forget all my worries
As love takes me away
As you bite my lip
Passionate and real
I shiver slightly
At the heat I feel
Mmmmm your kiss
Is like a lover's potion
Stealing my heart
And all my devotion!

TIM RIDSDALE

The sound of your voice
The kiss of your lips
The joy in your laugh
The sway of your hips
The look in your eyes
The feelings I feel
The warmth in my heart
Tells me it's real
Your messy hair
Your contagious laugh
Your crazy dance
You choreograph
The things I miss
When we're apart
I carry with me
Safe in my heart!

WHIMSICAL SENSATIONS

My spine tingles
At your gentle touch
Caressing my hair
That you do so much
I long for these moments
When I am away
Your sweet caresses
The things you don't say
Those quiet times
When words aren't needed
When our warmth is shared
When our eyes they pleaded
For time to stand still
To be lost in the moment
To honor our feelings
In love's bestowment
When your hair is messy
And you're a little shy
Lost in your eyes
My soul will fly
Whether early morning
Or along our way
The way you touch me
Makes my day!

TIM RIDSDALE

Dreams sweet dreams
Floating through my day
Tender sweet fantasies
Painted through a life of grey
Although we've never met
We have walked a million miles
Down many different paths
Holding hands and sharing smiles
The sky is a different shade
Each time we walk along
The conversations are endless
Among the birds of song
Your eyes are so amazing
With a hint of laughter there
I find myself drowning
In the simple depth of a stare
There are times we walk in silence
When no words are needed
A wave of feeling rushes in
And a hint of love is seeded
Then another dream will start
Which leads into another
Intoxicating, your every move
What a beautiful way to smother.

WHIMSICAL SENSATIONS

As I watch you sleep
I tried to remember
Me before you
Just as faint as an ember
My evenings in solitude
My mornings alone
A colorless world
As cold as stone
The laughs were few
The smiles even less
The tender longings
For anther's caress
The beauty all around
I dreamt I would share
The one who would answer
My most soulful prayer
The rest has faded
Lost in the night
Replaced by your love
And amazing delight
Now here as I watch you
The words are so few
To explain who I was
Me before you!

TIM RIDSDALE

My first desire
When I open my eyes
Is to see you near me
To hear your sighs
You make my day
So very much brighter
You lift my mood
Until it's so much lighter
And if we don't talk
Until the setting sun
I know that's where we'll meet
And I'll hold you Hun!
Because the last thing
I wish to remember
When closing my eyes
Is our love's eternal ember
That glows in your eyes
That flows through your touch
That I will protect
Because it means so much.

WHIMSICAL SENSATIONS

I will think of you
Until I hear your voice
Then my soul is soothed
For my heart to rejoice
I will think of you
Until you are near
When I feel your touch
And warm fuzzies appear
I will think of you
Until we share a kiss
That warms my life
And creates sheer bliss
I will think of you
In every way
How my life with you
Is beautiful each day.

TIM RIDSDALE

How does a heart endure
How does it wish to explain
With only a wave of emotion
For its love to truly sustain
How does our soul breathe
How does it open and close
It's the mystical part of love
That surprises us all I suppose
How is our brain so engaged
That it loses all sense of reason
Each time it's flooded through
When love is ripe in season
Maybe love is the why
That allows us to really live
As it stimulates all it touches
When we are so tentative
Or maybe love is amazing
With no words to compare
Because it's meant for two
It's beauty made to share.

WHIMSICAL SENSATIONS

Laying with you
Cuddled up to my chest
Feeling the warmth
Of your body's request
Your gentle sweet touch
Your soft gentle kiss
It's so easy to drop
Into love's beautiful abyss
Your love is incredible
Your voice is serene
You make me feel
Like when I was a teen
You give me your trust
And I know right away
How special this moment
That nothing can betray
The hearts of two people
Giving all of themselves
Is more magical in time
Than a library's shelves
It's a feeling we struggle
To explain or advise
But it's always there smiling
In the glow of our eyes!

TIM RIDSDALE

Your love powers my universe
Infused with all your passion
It leaves me always longing
For a beautiful extra ration
Moving through my life
You change my dreary days
Bringing a splash of color
In all your amazing ways
You make me feel like dancing
Like jumping in jubilation
You've reinvented my soul
Through love's reincarnation
I can't explain the joy
That fills me in every way
But I know down deep inside
I'm changing every day
To a man who wears a smile
To a man who knows elation
To a man whose heart's awakened
And filled with adoration.

WHIMSICAL SENSATIONS

The first thing I think about
When I start my day
Is you my love
In the strongest way
Lying beside you
I feel your heartbeat
Calling me closer
To where our lips meet
The powerful elation
Of our souls' connection
Recharges my body
In quiet perfection
To work all day
With thoughts of you
Brings me home with a smile
To a love that is true.

TIM RIDSDALE

The best medicine is tenderness
A single drop a day
On every word we share
Along our journey's way
It's a wonderful condition
That makes things brighter
Fills our lives with warmth
And we feel a little lighter
It makes life tastier
With the right amount of spice
There is no special recipe
So no need to be precise
Just fill your world with tenderness
Let kindness lead the way
Love will sow the seeds
That eventually save the day!

WHIMSICAL SENSATIONS

With you I talk
Until our voices are hoarse
And the joy I feel
Plots a whole new course
We all have a fairy tale
Tucked away in our hearts
With that perfect someone
Who's the sum of all parts
Of all our fantasies
And every dream
That fuels our passion
To some extreme
But when they walk into our life
With unimaginable zeal
It rewrites all our plans
And all that we feel
To be just as I am
With an amazing you
Makes everything fit
In a way nothing can subdue.

TIM RIDSDALE

Love is much more
Than words can express
Much more than the passion
Your soul can possess
Love is more than the action
Of raw true feeling
It's more than the butterflies
When a kiss sends us reeling
Love is more than your touch
And gentle caress
It's more than trust
And tender faithfulness
It's more than our strength
When woven together
Stronger and lighter
Than an eagle's feather
But when all these things
Are blended into one
We come as close to defining
Our love as anyone!

WHIMSICAL SENSATIONS

Actions speak volumes
To another's soul
They reach into their hearts
As love becomes whole
I may tremble at your touch
I may shiver from your kiss
But when we're apart
These things I miss
I may bring you flowers
To see your eyes glow
I may rub your sore muscles
Soft and slow
I may dance with you
In the strangest places
I may lighten your workday
To stay in good graces
But the things I do
That make you smile
Warm my heart
With all that's worthwhile.

TIM RIDSDALE

Your tired giggles
Your sleepy words
Make me think of counting
Shepherd's herds
Your cute little sighs
Your well-fought yawn
Like a lady warrior
From the Amazon
Your hazel eyes
As soft as a deer
Steal my heart
And make my year
But it's when you snuggle
Deeper into my arms
That you really show
All your sleepy-time charms!

WHIMSICAL SENSATIONS

Somehow you make my desire
More greedy for you
Unable to resist your beauty
That flows so easily through
Every inch of my body and soul
Your beauty gently caresses me
With a warm boldness
Driving away my doubts
And that lonely coldness
My heart beats faster
As I approach my queen
Tired muscles aching
From the day's labor unseen
All forgotten, energy renewed
When your eyes smile
How amazing you are
In your own sensual style
Waiting patiently for my return
To renew our love's desire
To feel our hearts beat wildly
Like a locomotive's fire
All that I do each day
Is to bring me back to you
To your extraordinary love
For my life to steadily imbrue.

TIM RIDSDALE

The sound of your voice
Is like the sweetest song
I can't remember a time
Before you came along
That I felt this happy
Just to listen in bliss
And dream of contentment
That's sealed with your kiss
The sound of your voice
Puts me at ease
Inviting you in
To do as you please
Your touch is so soft
And lovingly tender
I melt in your warmth
And totally surrender
The sound of your voice
Is a velvety array
That touches my soul
And brightens my day
You maybe don't think
I listen intently
But you wrap me all up
Ever so gently.

WHIMSICAL SENSATIONS

Moonlight on water
Reflecting like glass
Hiding the depth
Of its extraordinary mass
Put your hand in mine
And we'll walk in the night
To the water's edge
Under the full moon's light
The sand's still warm
Against our skin
My delicate caress
Is silky and thin
Soft wet kisses
Gentle to place
Passion igniting
For two hearts to race
Subtle moans
Soaked up in the waves
Our souls know
What each other craves
Our passion drives us
Deep into the night
Exhaustion finds us
In the morning light
Wrapped up in my arms
I feel your heartbeat
Content in the feeling
Of love's unwavering heat.

TIM RIDSDALE

Here I am
Standing in your door
Heart on my sleeve
Wanting more
I am riding on faith
And full of hope
Trying to navigate
Life's slippery slope
I have seen your eyes
For they have brought me here
Enveloped me whole
Discarding my fear
Will you be the one
Who decides my fate
Will you be the one
Who is my soulmate.

WHIMSICAL SENSATIONS

When I think of love
I think of beautiful things
Couples in love
Exchanging of rings
I see quiet walks
And smiling faces
Spectacular views
From exotic places
When I think of love
I see Venus and Mars
People making wishes
On falling stars
When I think of love
I see lovers kissing
Reminding me now
Of all I am missing
When I think of love
I see only you
Your eyes full of joy
And tenderness too
When I think of love
I see you and me
Walking together
Down by the sea
when I think of love
I think of forever
Of our souls intertwined
To hold us together.

TIM RIDSDALE

My mind it wonders
As I watch the night sky
Counting the stars
With no end, but I try
As they wink so slowly
I compare them to eyes
Some brighter, some smaller
Always constant as I turn by
I am waiting patiently
For that one falling flash
To ask for my wish
Before it turns into ash
In its last flash of glory
Would it permit me just one
To realize a dream
That my heart has spun
My dream is simple
My wants are not great
I present my small wish
To the hands of fate
My heart it pleads
As I ask to be whole
To find me the other
Who was joined to my soul.

WHIMSICAL SENSATIONS

Someday somewhere
I know we will meet
Introduced by friends
Or accidentally on the street
Recognizing immediately
By the look in our eyes
Or the accidental contact
As goosebumps arise
And from that day forward
Inseparable we'll remain
No matter what happens
We'll weather life's strain
You were born for me
I was born for you
Our souls were destined
For each other to pursue
But everything will come
When it will come
We'll find each other
By out hearts' gentle thrum
And in my arms
You'll find your peace
In a wave of emotion
In love's sweet caprice.

TIM RIDSDALE

I wish you were here
As your memory lingers
I feel your warmth
On the tips of my fingers
My old t-shirt
Stashed under my pillowcase
Still holds your scent
That I longingly embrace
I can feel your arms
And your breath on my chest
Long into the night
Where my mind won't rest
Your memory abounds
Throughout my days
Still showing me love
And how you amaze
From the depth of my soul
To my heart's sullen ache
I'm lost in your dream
Yet fully awake.

WHIMSICAL SENSATIONS

In only a blanket
You came to me
To wrap me up
And set passion free
My skin was warm
From the shower's heat
But yours was hotter
Soft and sweet
The kiss of your lips
Brought wild sensations
Filled with an array
Of bold temptations
We danced in the light
Of a spring sunset
Sharing a love
We'd never forget
The beauty of youth
Is to live in the moment
Never living in fear
Of the devil's component
But to experience joy
In its purest formation
Rippling through life
With a powerful vibration.

TIM RIDSDALE

You haunt my thoughts
In the most loving way
Filling my world
Improving my day
In the deep of the night
We share our dreams
Filled with passion
Bursting at the seams
But through my day
Nothing can compare
To all my wishes
With you I would share
You are my center of life
My fountain of youth
My sensual dream
My sweet loving truth
That fills my days
And consumes my nights
Filling my soul
With heavenly delights.

WHIMSICAL SENSATIONS

The wind whispers your name
And in my soul I tremble
A soft gentle ache
Begins to assemble
The need in my body
Burns with desire
To feel your touch
To be set afire
I feel your kiss
Burn deep in my skin
Your breath still hot
As my world starts to spin
The softness of your words
Ring true in my heart
Releasing the lion
Before I come apart
That feeling of freedom
To be totally wild
Where our love lay dormant
It is now reconciled
Can you feel these feelings
Pulsating through you
An intoxicating wine
That leaves you askew
I toss and I turn
As thoughts turn to dreams
Another long restless night
Lost in love's extremes.

TIM RIDSDALE

In this amazing life
The heavens grant us choice
So many paths to follow
So many things to voice
The wanderlust I've known
Deep in my restless soul
Always looking onward
Never within my control
The adventurous spirit there
Has taken me exotic places
Bringing me many friends
And beautiful smiling faces
But then I met an angel
Who redefined what's real
Opening another world
Where words begin to feel
Where my angel's gentle way
Filled my lonely mind
With thoughts of only her
So our souls could be combined
She is my summer moon
An amazing sensual version
To bask in your eyes
In love's total immersion
I never know what awaits
Or where new roads lead today
But I know where my love's given
And in whose arms I'll always stay.

WHIMSICAL SENSATIONS

You are my spring blossom
Refreshing and new
My window to Heaven
For which I look through
You are my robin's song
So tenderly sweet
You are my fragrant meadow
Where I wish to meet
You are my tropic island
I'm your ocean deep
You are my shining princess
I'm your castle keep
You fill my dreams
Until my soul overflows
Like the vastness of Heaven
Our love only grows.

TIM RIDSDALE

Love begins with a look
With affection in our eyes
That passionate look
No one can disguise
It leads to a kiss
So tender and real
Soft and enigmatic
Incredible to feel
The brush of a hand
Softly on skin
A feeling of butterflies
Will quickly begin
The quiver of lips
The tremble of hands
The chemical reaction
That no one understands
The passion ignited
That soulful ache
That pulses through us
When our bodies quake
Loves creates the impossible
So incredibly pure
That gives us the strength
In this life to endure!

WHIMSICAL SENSATIONS

The depth of your eyes
Leaves me quite bewitched
Drowning in your beauty
I'm totally transfixed
As your warmth engulfs me
I shiver and ache
The emotion fills me
As our souls awake
The first touch of your lips
Is gentle and warm
Only hints in your eyes
Of the passionate storm
The softness of your body
As it glides over mine
Gives way to a trust
For our hearts to entwine
The pulsations are as vivid
As the need in your eyes
We laid down as two
But only one will arise
Two hearts become one
Two souls are enchanted
In a love for all time
So rarely is granted.

TIM RIDSDALE

It's who you are inside
That makes me love you so
An amazing hidden diamond
That brightly wants to glow
Your funny sense of humor
And toughness is an act
Meant to hide a gentle heart
For true love to extract
A rare exquisite beauty
That leaves my heart in awe
Your soul it shines above
Breaking Heaven's laws
Your eyes may be the windows
To this very special place
But it's your smile and warmth
That makes me long for your embrace!

WHIMSICAL SENSATIONS

To be filled with joy
To feel your warmth like a flood
Coursing through me
Like my lifeblood
You are not afraid
To bare your soul
To me who would cherish it
And my heart to extol
To know the taste
Of your sweet lips
Safely stored away
In memory's grip
To know where truth
And passion meet
Bound by the sound
Of a single heartbeat
To find happiness
Warm and tender
To bask in its fullness
And amazing splendor
To protect it always
Like a newborn child
So I can finally live
With you beguiled.

TIM RIDSDALE

Our forehead's touch
As I caress your cheek
The warmth we feel
Needs no words to speak
Your hand on my heart
As I hold you close
It gently opens to you
Like an evening primrose
Your arms circle my waist
As your eyes search mine
For that passionate fire
That begins to shine
I could stare for hours
And get lost in your smile
Drift off in your eyes
And just float there a while
Before kissing your lips
A little bit of Heaven
That flutters my heart
And lets my soul start to leaven
The subtle changes
You invoke in my life
Makes me want you more
To become my wife!

WHIMSICAL SENSATIONS

You are my ocean of mystery
That has invited me in
Like a beautiful sunset
Or a sweet song of a violin
How do I explain
That you are part of me
That most gentle gift
Wrapped in sensuality
Like a leaf on the wind
You spin me around
In a dance with my soul
Your love is unbound
You warm my soul
Bringing life to my heart
Such a beautiful thing
You've given a start
So when I think of you
For the 1 millionth time
I'm lost for words
I've run out of rhythm
But I'll use the next
50 years, my beauty
To love you so sweetly
Until death steals my duty.

TIM RIDSDALE

Love isn't something dismissed
It's not something that we choose
It's not something that dies
Or can be used in a ruse
Love is found within us
It's in everything all around
It's stronger than iron
It never breaks down
We may give up on love
But it never gives up on us
Love is always the truth
And never treasonous
Love can be unpredictable
It can be sexy and mysterious
It can fill us with joy
And leave us delirious
Love is the only why
In sunshine and pain
It lives right through us
To always remain.

WHIMSICAL SENSATIONS

My sweet nymph of the woods
I long for your touch
Like fire and ice
You taunt me so much
With the sun at your back
You glide through the trees
The sight of your elegance
Floats with the breeze
Your eyes beckon me closer
To make you all mine
Two souls wrapped up
As our bodies entwined
We lay in the leaves
A dance of our fashion
Sharing our souls
Feeding our passion
You are all that I want
I am all that you need
For two hearts to live
Like they've just been freed.

TIM RIDSDALE

My mind is overwhelmed
By all thoughts of you
It's impossible to hide
The things that are true
Those moments when love
Radiates its unearthly light
It's impossible to hide
Exposed in full sight
I'm embracing this fever
Burning hot in my soul
So enticing its passion
It's too much to control
The thought of your lips
And your sensuous kiss
Floods all of my dreams
As I fall into remiss
The warmth you create
Pulls my body apart
Filling every last cell
Passing straight through my heart!

WHIMSICAL SENSATIONS

I want to whisper in your ear
All my crazy thoughts
Kiss you all over
To find your ticklish spots
I want to draw words on your back
With a caressing hand
That takes you away
Into a steamy dreamland
I want to place some ice cream
Across your chest
Lick it all off slowly
Until you are totally obsessed
I want to hold you close
Until we melt into one
Play lovers' games
Until the morning sun
I want to feel your heart
Beat against my lips
And feel all your shivers
From my fingertips
I want to fill your thoughts
With passion and lust
Ignite your desires
Until we both combust!

TIM RIDSDALE

Who makes your heart beat faster
Who makes your lips burn hot
Who makes your fingers tremble
Who makes your stomach knot
Who drives your deepest passion
Who ignites your wildest dreams
Who leaves you feeling dizzy
Who leaves you bursting at the seams
I know who makes my body ache
And fills me through and through
It's the one who twins my soul
And it has always been you

WHIMSICAL SENSATIONS

How lovely your eyes
Shine back at me
I'm lost in the depths
Of their deep blue sea
Your smile precedes
The warmth of your soul
That brings me joy
That's beyond control
Your gentle caress
And soft sweet kiss
Lifts my heart
In exquisite bliss
A loving whisper
A kiss on the cheek
Deep in my soul
You placed your mystique
You are my forever
My delicate flower
My friend, my lover
My finest hour!!

TIM RIDSDALE

Heart of yours
Piece of mine
Completes a love
When souls align
Heart of truth
Heart of gold
Nothing so strong
Nothing so bold
Heart so tender
Full of joy
Creating a happiness
For two to enjoy
Hearts that long
For our loving twin
Soulmates forever
Joined from within
Hearts that feel
Deeper with time
Like a gentle wisp
Of a dream so sublime
Hearts that stand
Together in strength
That nothing can strain
Or yield at length.

WHIMSICAL SENSATIONS

How long in me
A loneliness has grown
To the depths of my soul
Like nothing I've known
I search for the love
That would set me free
Expand in my heart
That has been an absentee
A sweet spring flower
To ease my blues
With love to share
And a warmth to infuse
For one great love
That would give us wings
To soar to the freedom
Of more meaningful things
To ignite a passion
Giving loneliness its death
From the sound of your voice
And the heat of your breath
The softness of your kiss
The smoothness of your skin
And the love that I dream of
Trapped deep within.

TIM RIDSDALE

It's a magical thing
What you do to me
To make me dream
Of the love I see
If you were a diamond
I'd be your jeweler
If I was a knight
You'd be my ruler
For love is a noble act
Offering faith and trust
To humbly give to another
Your heart and soul's a must
To need another's love
As much as they need yours
Is the only way that heaven
Will open up its doors
To bless a life together
For two souls to intertwine
To be each other's strength
In the truth of God's design.

WHIMSICAL SENSATIONS

Before we go
Let me taste your lips
And trace your face
With my fingertips
Kiss your neck
And breathe in your scent
Hold you in my arms
Where my heart is content
Until the next time we meet
And again we are one
Immersed in each other
Where love can't be undone
To tremble and to feel
The heat of our passion
Enveloped by its heat
In overwhelming fashion
So before we go
Let me taste your lips
And trace your face
With my fingertips!

TIM RIDSDALE

A deep breath
A strong hug
Senses buzzing
Like an expensive drug
Coursing through me
With every beat
Igniting my body
In a dizzying heat
Wild shivers
Pulsating flashes
Through my muscles
Like 20 lashes
Exploring tongue
Over quivering lips
Gentle touches
From fingertips
Soft moans
Wanting eyes
Undress me slowly
Of any disguise
Raw love
Souls laid bare
Total submission
For hearts to share!

WHIMSICAL SENSATIONS

Sometimes it's better
When we don't speak
But just lay with you
In love's mystique
No words wasted
No empty promises
No hollow thoughts
Or doubting Thomas
Just you and me
In love's embrace
Bodies smolder
In our happy place
Where we can be us
In love's gentle grace
Where our souls intertwine
In our hearts' time and space
So it's not really silence
As I look into your eyes
But a symphony from within
That your beauty will reprise.

TIM RIDSDALE

In the heat of the day
Or coolness of the night
You have slowly become
My heart's delight
You refresh my soul
You taught me to cope
With great expectation
You filled me with hope
For an early sunrise
Or the beauty at sunset
You opened my eyes
And I'm forever in your debt
To see what is real
to strip away lies
To feel again
By breaking all ties
In your warmth
I have found
Your tender heart
Such a peaceful sound
Its greatest gift
Is a place to belong
That rings true in my soul
Like the sweetest song!

WHIMSICAL SENSATIONS

You are my gentle storm
In the evening heat
My welcome relief
My much-needed treat
Your love awakens me
In the midst of your downpour
Healing my soul
Making me reach for more
As I look into your eyes
And watch your moves
There's a gentle storm
That my love approves
Your smile, it warms me
My emptiness fades
All those sacred feelings
Begin a passionate cascade
Look into my eyes
And tell me what you need
Against my strong shoulder
Let the loneliness concede
Let's dream together
The most breathtaking moment
That we never forget
As love's wildest proponent.

TIM RIDSDALE

The wave of a butterfly
The kiss of the sea
Your passionate touch
And what it means to me
Soft caress of a breeze
That plays with your hair
The feeling of flying
When I'm caught in your stare
The warmth of the sun
The vastness of the skies
Does not compare
To what your love exemplifies
The strength of a river
The power of hope
Your incredible faith
Reflects like a kaleidoscope
The soft touch of a baby
The trust in their eyes
I feel this in you
When you share your butterflies
You bedazzle my soul
You make my heart sigh
You are the bough
To which my love is tied.

WHIMSICAL SENSATIONS

I'm carelessly free
As I sing a song
To my heart's beat
As I move along
The sky is like a flower
Blossoming deep red
In the evening sun
Like a brilliant poppy bed
Reminding me of the wounds
And scars in each place
But with quiet determination
I seek God's face
I accept my fate
Laying my soul bare
Against life's torments
To take your heart and share
This love between us
So fragile and meek
To gladly let it grow
Into all we both seek.

TIM RIDSDALE

Love needs to be a mystery
Not planned and known
It should fill us with wonder
Not rules to be shown
It should develop from tenderness
From passion of living
From a place of grace
Understanding and forgiving
Love can't be bought
Or built on a lie
No rules of engagement
Our hearts must comply
In its infancy stage
Love is fragile and weak
But powerful and strong
when it reaches its peak
You may search all you want
And pray for relief
But love will not come
Unless you drown in belief
At your most vulnerable point
It will rush in on a wave
So don't ever settle
Be open and brave
Love will fill your soul
The way God intended
So you let down your walls
Leave them undefended.

WHIMSICAL SENSATIONS

The smell of fall
Is in the evening air
Cooler breezes swirl
Crisply through my hair
The warmth of summer fades
With the last rays of the day's sun
The changing leaves
Give way to Indian summer's run
A most romantic time
For me to be with you
Love seeks my ravaged soul
That your passion may imbrue
A gentle kiss
With a soft caress
Brings our bodies
To the point of coalesce
To let our hearts
Grow strong together
Giving that feeling
Of light as a feather
That tells me dance
In the midst of confusion
Breaking the mysteries
Of all love's illusions.

TIM RIDSDALE

Listening to nature's symphony
Sitting on the steps with you
Neither of us saying a word
Just listening to all the ado
The wind sets the tempo
With a soothing rustle of the leaves
A robin adds her voice
From underneath the eaves
The bees buzz from flower to flower
Dancing along the pond
A butterfly flutters by
Like the wave of a conductor's wand
A cricket sounds off
As evening has begun
As the black fly zooms home
To beat the setting sun
The frogs start a chorus
In tune with the cricket's call
The robins fall silent
As shadows start to sprawl
I wrap my arms around you
My warmth against your back
We sit a little longer
Listening to God's soundtrack!

WHIMSICAL SENSATIONS

Can you kiss me
To wake me from this loneliness
The touch of your lips
So perfect and harmonious
Their tender heat
Awakens my soul
Makes my knees feel weak
Like a newborn foal
My eyes will open
And search for yours
You snuggle closer
As my hand explores
The back of your neck
And through your hair
Our foreheads touch
Locked in love's prayer
It seems like a dream
Lying there with you
Our hearts are full
Their beats on cue
The smell of coffee
Brings me back
To your intoxicating kiss
Like a sweet cognac
You've awakened me now
As your eyes sparkle and blaze
Igniting our passions
In an incredible haze.

TIM RIDSDALE

How can you look
More beautiful to me everyday
Lifting my heart
In so gentle a way
Your inner world
You open to me
Your amazing world
I think all would agree
A passionate lover
A devoted mother
A twin to my soul
Like I've known no other
You are the yin
To my yang
So when we're apart
I get a loving pang
For your eternal beauty
And your heartbeat's sound
And your warmth from within
That my soul has found!

WHIMSICAL SENSATIONS

Love is like a butterfly
So fragile and weak
Yet oh so beautiful
And tender and unique
When given freely
From deep within
Our hearts they flutter
And our souls they spin
Like the wings of a butterfly
We gracefully take flight
The power of its passion
Gives strength to its height
And we soar to the heavens
On the wings of God's gift
Given a happiness
So true and swift
If we give all of ourselves
To ride this whirlwind
On the wings of a butterfly
Our souls can be twinned.

TIM RIDSDALE

You are my joy
And also my pain
My morning sun
And my evening rain
You are so far away
Yet I hold you close inside
You turn my heart to wishing
For what my soul decides
Do you think of me
When you open your eyes
Do you feel my touch
In memory's disguise
Do lips burn
With love's desire
Or do these thoughts
Leave you in mire
Goosebumps form
When I think of you
Your hot wet kiss
My feelings anew
When you do the things
We used to do
Do they seem mundane
And quite askew
Is your life still happy
Or missing that thing
That allows you to blossom
Like flowers in spring.

WHIMSICAL SENSATIONS

I want to take your hand
And lead you into my world
And let our passion and love
Be wildly unfurled
We'll search our souls
Until we find
That we are as one
Body, soul, and mind
Will you share with me
All your desires
To quench your thirst
Of passion's fires
You can call me handsome
And all that adores
But all I want to hear
Is that I am only yours.

TIM RIDSDALE

The immeasurable power of love
And all it can endure
Is really quite incredible
That it remains so very pure
It knows when your soul is ready
And like a starburst of inspiration
It draws another to you
Without time for negotiation
When reality crashes into dreams
It's never by design
Love explodes through our bodies
With feelings so divine
Our hearts are beating faster
Our bodies tense and shiver
Kisses burn with passion
For the joy that love delivers
It's worse than getting sick
But worth more than stores of gold
And we'll give everything we are
For the chance to have and hold.

WHIMSICAL SENSATIONS

Gazing out into the black night
Listening to the rain fall
Watching distant flashes of lighting
Give light to the passing squall
I feel you in my heart tonight
Like many lonely nights before
Returning to me
For our love to restore
That passion I'm missing
That only you fully ignite
No matter the day
Or time of night
Whether it's dark
Or under the full moon's light
The strength of our love
Penetrates all, to my delight
Feeling the passion of your lips
From so many miles away
Giving my life meaning
On life's highway
So that even on the darkest night
Hope flickers its loving light
Giving faith to my dreams
And strength to continue to fight!

TIM RIDSDALE

Meeting you there
Alone together in that moment
Your eyes carried me away
Showing me life's missing component
Your voice was like sweet nectar
Filling every inch of my being
Igniting my soul
With pure feeling
My heart beating faster
As words failed me
Managing only a quick smile
As my mind leapt free
Thinking of a first hug
A first kiss
The softness of your lips
Wrapping me up in gentle bliss
A gift from God
An angel for sure
An inspiring lady
With so much allure
20 seconds of courage
Is all I need
To truly meet her
When a heart's been freed.

WHIMSICAL SENSATIONS

The beauty I see
Not of this world
But hidden within
Adorned and imperiled
No words to express
Only the look in my eyes
To open your beauty
You so eloquently disguise
You are my miracle
A blessing from God
Your amazing light
Shows you're not a facade
We feel each other
Through precious time
Held apart by distance
And love's paradigm.

TIM RIDSDALE

I think of you
As I touch my lips
The feel of your kiss
As I come to grips
I think of love
As I touch my lips
Staring deep in your eyes
With my hands on your hips
I feel your passion
As I touch my lips
The warmth of your body
Caresses my fingertips
I feel your heartbeat
As I touch my lips
Remembering soft kisses
That makes mine skip
I remember the wetness
As I touch my lips
So sweet and desired
My soul it flips
I remember it all
As I touch my lips
We passed in the night
Like two voyaging ships.

WHIMSICAL SENSATIONS

The taste of your lips
The scent of your hair
Your skin against mine
The passion lovers share
Your gentle caress
The solace of my bed
A reminder of hope
That dances in my head
The thoughts of games
That lovers play
The feelings that linger
The words I would say
The gift of love
Eluded only by time
A faithful seeker
Of love's soulful crime
That steals my heart
That seals my fate
To flounder in bliss
With no advocate.

TIM RIDSDALE

I want to whisper softly
How much I want you
Let the past drift away
For the creation of new
To share with you
My stores of tenderness
My wounded heart
And soulful caress
I want to feel your lips
Hot against mine
Your building desire
When your inner beauty shines
I want to share with you
My strongest lust
My loving faith
My hope and trust
I want to feel your locks
Of long flowing hair
With tender touches
That your heart would ensnare
Can we feel together
Write our own love song
Build a life together
Beautiful and strong.

WHIMSICAL SENSATIONS

I wish I was the wind
To create a light breeze
To caress you skin
To tickle and tease
To playfully toss
The locks of your hair
To stroke your cheek
In a life-long affair
To cool your lips
To whisper in your ear
To wrap you up
To totally endear
I may lift your skirt
Like a naughty schoolboy
To caress your legs
What a dangerous ploy
I may lick your body
With a passionate gust
To caress your soul
And test your trust
But alas the wind
Cannot give me the bliss
Of the flesh and blood
Of your heavenly kiss.

TIM RIDSDALE

The beauty of the dawn
Brings all that is good
That enriches my soul
The way nothing else could
When the rays of the sun
Spread across the room
Your beauty like a flower
Blossoms in full bloom
The warmth of your body
Close against mine
Soothes my heart
By love's design
The warmth of your breath
The fullness of your lips
Soft on my neck
When my heartbeat skips
I feel a splash of joy
When you open your eyes
And lost in their depths
They hypnotize
In that moment so real
You are my confidant
All I have wished for
All I could want!!

WHIMSICAL SENSATIONS

We lay awake in our bed
Listening to the night sounds
While deep in our hearts
The magic of love abounds
Our naked bodies pressed into each other
In the warmth of our tender embrace
Feeling the velvety hand
Of God's amazing grace
I feel your warm breath
And hear your contented sigh
Your eyelashes kissing me softly
Like the wings of a butterfly
I search for your lips
Pressing them hot against mine
Sending wild pulses through me
So exquisitely divine
Our fingertips explore
All our touch observes
Etched into memory
All your body's curves
I inhale your every scent
Absorbing softly every sound
Feeling you in my soul
With each breath you're tightly wound
I have fallen deeply in love
Like a child's first touch from their mother
I won't, I can't, my lady
Ever think of loving another.

TIM RIDSDALE

I saw love today
Two children sharing bliss
A simple act of kindness
Brought about their first sweet kiss
I saw love today
As a retired couple walked
Hand-in-hand side-by-side
Giggling as they talked
I saw love today
In two young lovers' embrace
Saying goodbye before parting
With sadness in their face
I saw love today
Her little face aglow
New experiences with her Momma
Her love as pure as snow
I saw love today
When I looked into your eyes
Its warmth filled my heart
As I felt my soul reprise
I saw love today
With a promise for my life
That you would share it with me
As my best friend and wife!!

WHIMSICAL SENSATIONS

We have met in our dreams
A thousand ways
Our souls preceded us
Throughout this maze
As our worlds collided
You became my muse
Into my heart
You were able to transfuse
An elegant Lady
A delicate lover
My soulmate forever
I would soon discover
The heat from your kiss
Your passion to behold
The softness of your touch
Takes me to the threshold
You may only be mine
When I close my eyes
For the distance between us
Disappears by love's devise
So until we meet
Until I feel your touch
My love will seek you
That I've longed so much.

TIM RIDSDALE

As the sun gently pours out
Its warm rays across the room
Promising another amazing day with you
For our love affair to resume
In the quiet of the kitchen
Making coffee for two
Your beauty fills the room
Like a symphony's debut
Your soft touch
And gentle way
Drawing me to you
As our hearts play
My soul seeking yours
For its love to give
Committing to memory
Every moment we live
Our love is boundless
As we work at it as one
No matter the frustration
Our love is never undone
Distance cannot separate us
As time strengthens our bond
Our happiness inspires
As our hearts become more fond
I am forever yours
And you will always be mine
It's Love in its simplicity
So easy to define!!

WHIMSICAL SENSATIONS

I toss and turn
While I lie awake
Without you here
For passion's sake
These nights alone
Are filled with loss
Our empty bed
I roll across
I try to sleep
As exhaustion pleads
But that's not what
My lonely heart needs
It longs for you
And your tender kiss
That lingers with me
Wrapped in bliss
My body aches
For your sweet embrace
Your gentle touch
I can't replace
I'm lost without you
In the turmoil of night
My soul is begging
With all its might
I'm half the man
I soon discover
Without the warmth
Of my precious lover!!

TIM RIDSDALE

You are my blessing
My love song
The words carry me away
As I sing along
You are my warmth
My rainy day lover
A precious treasure
For me to discover
You are my spring flower
My breath of fresh air
My daily dream
My sometime, somewhere
You read my mind
You inspire my hope
You are my view to the stars
My astronomical telescope
You are my world
You make everything right
You are the solid ground
For which I fight
You are the one I love
Without any excuses
My soul is open
To all your seduces
I am yours today
Tomorrow, forever
I ask for your heart
And your love's full measure!

WHIMSICAL SENSATIONS

The depth of your love
Is mysterious as the ocean
Invited into your harbor
With trust and devotion
With the promise of rest
For my soul to heal
You offered yourself
So humble and real
You drew me in closer
On your tide of emotion
Dispelling my fears
And preconceived notions
When I took your hand
Gently in mine
A new world opened up
That only our love could define
Now my eyes are on you
You are all that I need
Your amazing love
Holds my hearts deed!!

TIM RIDSDALE

The night I met you
I have no words to explain
My chest it struggled
For my heart to constrain
Your gentle caress
Gave way to my heart
Awakened my soul
As my walls fell apart
Like a warm summer wind
You lifted my mood
A refreshing warmth
To end my solitude
You opened your world
With laughter and care
Where two hearts could meet
With so much to share
I was humbled by you
By your inner world
So softly I tread
As around me it whirled
So amazing you are
Coming into my life
I can't imagine you otherwise
Than being my wife!!

WHIMSICAL SENSATIONS

Life is so beautiful
When you need only one thing
The true love of another
That flows like a wellspring
And an irresistible wish
That fills us with hope
Of love that is pure
For our hearts to elope
The burning desire
In another's eyes
The warmth of their care
Without compromise
The simplicity of a smile
As light as the breeze
The touch of two hands
Freely at ease
These things that we do
With our souls' intention
Are valued the most
As God's purest invention.

TIM RIDSDALE

Daring sensuality
Tender sweet dreams
Let love fall freely
Like the moon's gentle beams
Let your heart see
Through the soul of another
For there you transform
Into my one and only lover
Let passion absorb
The heat of our touch
Engulfing our bodies
For our love means so mush
Let your mind flow
With the feelings we share
To explore possibilities
That we only now dare
We are one and the same
In the strength of our trust
Together forever
Until we turn back to dust!!

WHIMSICAL SENSATIONS

What do you dream of
When you find yourself alone
What weighs your heart down
Like a great heavy stone
Is it a yearning for love
For the touch of another
To find that real soul
Before life starts to smother
Do you have enough faith
That you will persevere
To struggle and fight
When things are unclear
To hold onto that dream
To lift up your hope
To trust in another
For strength to both cope
I dream of a lady
That makes it all right
When I look in her eyes
I see a strong shining knight
Who makes me feel
Much deeper than any
Who holds my heart
And stands out from the many
She creates a world
I would die to protect
A world we both love
That to us is perfect!!

TIM RIDSDALE

The sigh of my heart
As my soul breathes deep
Can you feel its rhythm
In its passionate sleep
It waits for you
Your love so divine
So bright and tender
It's undefinable shine
I need your love
So pure and real
To hold you now
Your warmth I feel
When I see it in your eyes
I feel it in my soul
My heart it trembles
That I can't control
To dream together
Of our forever
To bring to life
Our someday, our whenever.

WHIMSICAL SENSATIONS

Our souls in the night
Search for each other
Aching with longing
That darkness can't smother
To be free to love
To dance among the stars
Leave loneliness behind
And take what is ours
What distance has held
And time has marched on
We'll cherish in our souls
Dancing until dawn
Was it a dream
No, the feelings linger
Like a sweet melody
Of a Sunday church singer
To carry me through
Each day apart
Until I close my eyes
And you fill my heart!!

TIM RIDSDALE

The eloquence of the world
Has become a silent advocate
For the soul's plea
For love's passion to emulate
And through your eyes
Engulfed by your dreams
Wrapped up in your warmth
Safe from extremes
Like a river of truth
That floods through my veins
Erasing my doubts
Until only your love remains
I am yours by faith
In your love I shall fill
Yours by my vow
To do with what you will.

WHIMSICAL SENSATIONS

Looking up at the stars
When we are apart
The long lonely night
The aching in my heart
We both talk to the moon
Who listens so well
So quiet and calm
For our stories to tell
I feel your touch
And hear your soft voice
Up there in the Heavens
Where angels rejoice
Your sweet gentle whisper
That gets into my soul
Makes a real man shiver
That your heart can control
Its strong steady beat
Like a beacon in the night
Calling me home
By its radiating light
So as we talk to the moon
And tell him our plight
His warm steady gaze
Reminds me what's right.

TIM RIDSDALE

One stolen look
At your carefree smile
Its sensual warmth
I'm so easily beguiled
And I wonder what
Is behind those eyes
A passionate soul
For my dreams to agonize
Their uncharted depth
So inviting to me
The call of adventure
No one can foresee
Another stolen look
And I'm caught in your glance
Locked up in your beauty
In a heavenly trance
Those warm fuzzy feelings
As butterflies take flight
No way to deny it
It's love at first sight.

WHIMSICAL SENSATIONS

There's a cool crisp winter wind
That's waiting at the door
That just can't deter our walks
That we simply both adore
Arm in arm we go
Your soul dancing free
My heart holding your warmth
With my love's guarantee
You see Love is not just a word
But a deeper warmth inside
A strong desire to protect
All we share with passion's tide
Our time together is precious
For our souls to reconnect
Letting our hearts' needs
Find the time for them to reflect
All those tender feelings
Expressed in our gentle kiss
That lifts my body's spirit
And saves me from the abyss.

TIM RIDSDALE

Close your eyes
And breathe with me
We'll bask in the warmth
Of our sensuality
Place your head
Gently on my chest
Feel the beat of my heart
Where my love is confessed
The warmth of our body
Expressed from your soul
Fills me with passion
That my love would extol
Each breath that I take
Brings me closer to you
Our universe opens
For our hearts to go through
To a place of our own
Where we share all our joy
To strengthen the ties
No one can destroy.

WHIMSICAL SENSATIONS

Alone now with my words
For you to gently embrace
The tenderness I share
In each word of grace
Each loving thought
Reaching out across
The endless space
Feeling every joy, every loss
I'm there with you
As I carry you in my heart
Protecting you
Every piece, every part
Giving warmth
And tender care
For our souls
To have a share
Until we are together again
Basking in our love
Where only you and I
Had the courage thereof.

TIM RIDSDALE

I long to look into your eyes
And see love there
So pure and sincere
Like a child unaware
Looking back at me
With nothing but trust
Safe in my care
In a world that's unjust
To feel your warmth
And gentle heartbeat
Against my skin
Like a burning heat
No words can describe
The feelings created
Or the deep connection
Our souls have articulated
But looking into your eyes
Locked in that moment
Changed forever by love
So powerful and potent
I would understand love's beauty
And its ability to make time stand still
Riding the tidal wave
In the wake of love's will.

WHIMSICAL SENSATIONS

We all find the courage
Sooner or later
To live our lives
As more than a spectator
To seek out a little sanctuary
Where we're willing to share
Where we're gentle and meek
And our hearts can care
Where loneliness fades
Where our passions burn long
And Fear has no power
Where our love stands strong
The price we've paid
To find this place .
The experience to recognize
Is written on our face
But nothing compares
To love's creation
When we find our place
Of pure elation.

TIM RIDSDALE

Remember love is a verb
And that's what the world is about
It leaves our soul searching
And our dreams so devout
We search for a friend
To share all our joys
To comfort each other
And give our life poise
We search for a lover
To share all our passion
Where our souls can flourish
And feelings aren't rationed
We search for our place
And a home that is good
Where we don't always agree
But we're always understood.

WHIMSICAL SENSATIONS

They say love is one thing
To be loved is another
That soft tender feeling
That starts with our mother
We bathe in its warmth
Such a beautiful thing
That fills our dreams
And makes our hearts sing
Love gives us strength
And allows us to trust
Builds a strong steady faith
And heals the unjust
To be loved by another
Is so exquisitely fine
It brings out a beauty
That makes our soul shine.

TIM RIDSDALE

What makes us afraid
What makes us believe
What draws us closer
What makes us leave
What ignites our passion
What warms our soul
What drives away demons
When our heart needs parole
What creates that scar
What challenges our mind
What heals our memories
What makes us defined
What makes us search
What's pure as a dove
The answer is easy
It's only real love.

WHIMSICAL SENSATIONS

Real love brings a tear
To a strong man's eye
Real love puts passion
In a true woman's sigh
Real love is reflected
In a young child's face
Real love is a gift
That teaches us grace
Real love is not found
But rather finds you
Real love is the essence
For our souls to pursue
Real love fills our hearts
In the darkest of night
Real love conquers all
When we come to the light
Real love is amazing
It's life's greatest enhancer
Real love is the truth
When we don't know the answer.

TIM RIDSDALE

You touch me so
To affect me profoundly
Your soft silky touch
Leaves me sleeping unsoundly
You give my body bliss
With each caress of your hand
The sweet chorus of music
You easily command
Your words touch my soul
More tenderly than your hand
Leave my body in tremors
Unable to stand
As your eyes undress me
I'm captured with a kiss
No other could touch me
And affect me like this!

WHIMSICAL SENSATIONS

My dreams for you
Are always sunny
Gentle and kind
So Sweet like honey
When life gets cold
I'm your warmth and lover
Your umbrella in the rain
Your protection and cover
I'll hold you close
To keep you warm
With the strength in my soul
There can be no harm
So as I look out the window
As a strong wind blows
The storm rages on
In the absence of repose
I'll fight through the cloud
And reach for the sun
In the warmth of our love
That can't be undone.

TIM RIDSDALE

I close my eyes
And picture you smiling
Your warmth I feel
So magically beguiling
I hear your laugh
As your smile gets bigger
Sweet loving music
Delivered with vigor
Your shyness has passed
When You know I'll protect
All that we are
Where our souls reconnect
You challenge my morals
Which makes me stronger
To discard all the memories
Not needed any longer
Together our love
Has created a home
So peaceful a place
We call it Shalom.

WHIMSICAL SENSATIONS

You're always in my thoughts
Racing through my mind
Interrupting quiet time
I never seem to find
My heart is always restless
When my mind's askew
My soul is always longing
Forever wanting you
And when I try to work
My fingertips let me down
Remembering every touch
Until in emotion I slowly drown
Because my fingertips have memory
The sensations oh so real
Like you are right here with me
Your memory I can feel
And it moves so deep inside me
That I feel a little ache
As my fingertips remember
And my soul comes wide awake
I still feel the goosebumps
On skin caressed so slightly
And the softness of your hair
That I stroked so very lightly
The heat of love's elixir
Warms my very lips
But it's all the amazing memories
Drawn back through my fingertips.

TIM RIDSDALE

My love will shine
To light the way
For you through life
Each and every day
Your pretty smile
Will fuel that light
That glows from within
Steady and bright
Your warmth and kindness
Are never wasted
When the fruits of love
Are there to be tasted
Our respect and tenderness
Will grant us a world
Creating traditions
For our children to unfurl
You are all that I want
In this life and the next
You're are the epitome of passion
That all love reflects
I believe in no other
Like I believe in you
You are all that is good
And all that is true.

WHIMSICAL SENSATIONS

The sun spread across
The large stone balustrade
Outlining her feminine curves
Perfectly from where I laid
The wind played with her hair
To no real effect
Her warmth penetrated the room
And things felt entirely perfect
Getting out of bed
I wrapped my arms around her
Holding her close to my chest
Protecting her from any saboteur
For the first time I was content
And I felt completely whole
Wrapped up in love's armor
Where we were joined at the soul
Together looking out over the ocean
Our hearts beating in unison
Content in our future
Yet loving life for all its imperfection.

TIM RIDSDALE

We were two silhouettes
Alone in the dark
In the splinter of time
Caught up in love's spark
I did not want to wonder
What could have been
So I opened my soul
And let you come in
Now my fingers trace
The shape of your lips
In the failing light
As the moon dips
A passionate kiss
And a longing stare
All my senses were tingling
My emotions laid bare
We shared our feelings
And explored ourselves
Creating new memories
To fill our shelves
With a love that lasts
A lifetime and more
Creating an adventure
For two souls to adore.

WHIMSICAL SENSATIONS

Love comes softly
Undulating down
Like the wave of a whisper
I'm immersed in the sound
Love comes softly
With all its grace
Displacing all anger
At its own silky pace
Love comes softly
From the depths of the soul
All we need is trust
And faith to atoll
Love comes softly
To fully incite
And envelope me whole
In the truth of its light
Love comes softly.

TIM RIDSDALE

Add one cup of patience
And two more of love
A teaspoon of understanding
And a little purity of a dove
A tablespoon of touch
And a slice of romance
Two cups of hotness
To leave nothing to chance
Bring out the friendship
And add more than a cup
Think only kind thoughts
And mix it all up
Place in the oven
And smell goodness filling the room
Sprinkle in some children
And watch family bloom
There are many recipes
Two people can test
But this one's with love
So I like it the best

WHIMSICAL SENSATIONS

I found myself waiting
Though I said I would never
Waiting for something
Sometimes not so clever
Am I waiting on life
Or some substance thereof
Or something worth living for
And someone to love
I found myself waiting
Though I said I would never
One among millions
Caught up in forever
Behind my own mask
Away from public display
My loneliness blossoms
From romantic decay
I found myself waiting
Though I said I would never
Among all the faces
To continue my endeavor
To create some happiness
To give and receive
Waiting for the one
Because I believe.

TIM RIDSDALE

Love is a diamond
Reflecting all ways
In a million beams
Like a glowing haze
What love reflects
Is a tiny smile
Cuddles before bed
Making it all worthwhile
What love reflects
Is tender thoughts
From loving hearts
That God has taught
What love reflects
Are special days
Filled with emotion
Under another's gaze
What love reflects
Is hopes and dreams
That warm the soul
In all extremes
What love reflects
Is tender scenes
It's always there
And never demeans
What love reflects
Is all you are to me
As vast as the Sahara
As beautiful as the sea.

WHIMSICAL SENSATIONS

Beauty always catches the eye
Whether it glows like a ruby from within
Or shines like a diamond
In love's spiraling spin
It can bring out a smile
Along with one's charm
It can leave us feeling tingly
Or all sunny and warm
It's a wisp of wind
It's the morning dew
It's the changing of seasons
When everything's new
It's that helping hand
In our darkest hour
It's a gift from the heart
If only a single flower
It's the morning sunrise
Over our place of thought
It's that elusive wind
That sailors have sought
It's the simplest things
To the grandest invention
It's the perfect joke
That disperses the tension
It's a mother's first gaze
On her child of creation
It's basking in a pool
Of friendship's sensations
It's so many things
To so many each day
That the definition of beauty
Is really...for each of us to say.

TIM RIDSDALE

Standing there together
Alone in that one moment
I stared into the most intense eyes
And in their depths was wonderment
There was wisdom and understanding
An old soul but yet...
The enthusiasm of youth
Like none I have ever met
To look at life unbiased
Through her eyes
To see all of life's beauty
Would be a natural high
It would be as perfect
As if time stood still
Just long enough
To let two hearts fill
With all the wondrous feelings
That we experience by serendipity
And hold onto for the rest
Of our lives in marvelous simplicity.

WHIMSICAL SENSATIONS

Do you want to be kissed
In the most tender places
Slowly I'll place them
Until your heart races
I can kiss you endlessly
Or until we feel as one
With light feather touches
Until the morning sun
I'll let the whole world melt
As I unleash my love
An avalanche of desire
To be in awe of
What do you want
I want to be yours
Look into your eyes
For all they explore
See unquenchable fire
Captured by a kiss
To live for eternity
Creating loves bliss.

Printed in Canada